A Childs
Perspective
of a
Gay Parent

Beverly Nimke

BALBOA.PRESS

A DIVISION OF HAY HOUSE

Balboa Press books may be ordered through booksellers or by contacting:

Balboa Press
A Division of Hay House
1663 Liberty Drive
Bloomington, IN 47403
www.balboapress.com
844-682-1282

Print information available on the last page.

ISBN: 978-1-9822-5991-4 (sc)
ISBN: 978-1-9822-5992-1 (e)

Balboa Press rev. date: 12/09/2020

This book is dedicated to my mother,
my children and my husband James.

CONTENTS

INTRO

As I give my introduction I need to say I am not angry and I am not frustrated! Just very happy that I am able to discuss my experiences with the topic I wish to discuss. Homosexuality is a major topic and a very sensitive one if you will. I am not at liberty to discuss all of the major things in one's life that cause such a behavior. I only want to discuss my experience with it.

I am no way passing any human judgement on anyone or any specific person that I may have been in contact with. Only a child's perspective on how my life went through this wonderful journey we call life. One can say that this work can be a self-help book. One can say a peaceful look into a new journey of life, living and loving.

Amenra

CHAPTER 1

Were it all started "The Perfect Life"

As I sit and ponder the ideal of writing this book, my husband and I had a brief conversation. He looked at me and said when you are getting started; there is no reasons to ponder just get it done my love. I had to chuckle for a moment knowing he is right. Well it all began the year of 1964 January 17th that is when I was born. My mother and father were married for some time after that. What I thought as a perfect family me my mom and dad, my brothers all had a great life and an awesome family I thought at the time. Things were great, an awesome neighborhood, great food, beautiful home the works if you will. Well educated parents, holidays were always perfect. I remember my mom bust her ass off preparing what most people in America would dream of having for holiday meals.

Even without holidays the women was awesome in the kitchen. Amongst other things she was great! It's what people would call the American dream. Sometimes it's hard to talk to people in terms of my upbringing because of my background, i.e. economics and socialization process.

Some people really don't want to hear about all of the good things, perhaps things were different for them in terms of economics. But if I am to tell or write about what I wish to write about than all things must be discussed.

I have to say that being able to write this book makes me feel so much freedom that I never thought I had before. I need to add that I am in no way making fun of anyone or passing on any judgement. I just want to share my experience. My mother and father were very important to me. So when they divorced it was trauma. My father was like a prince to me and my mother his princess. Not anything out of the extraordinary of any other child growing up with their parents. I know that both of them loved me and my siblings very much so.

I sometimes sit and wonder what went wrong in their relationship. I know that nothing is perfect in any kind of relationship but I also know that if it is salvageable than it can work. I will not spend too much time on why it did not work for they, I guess we all have are faults. I remember as a child how we would all sit around the fire place and have our family time which that was awesome. My mother worked nights and my father worked during the day. So when he came home my younger brother and I would ride along with my dad to take my mother to work.

My mom always had dinner ready for us so that my father didn't have to do much but make sure we did homework and had dinner and had our baths. It really seemed very easy and perfect! At least it appeared we had it all. My mother and father of course like any other married couple had their issues. As children you stay out of your parents martial affairs if our smart. The only thing that should be observed is that you have all of the necessities as a child.

In my mind we had those things and then some. I never dreamed of losing my dad so young. It was like he just vanished off the earth, just like that! Gone! I remember most of the kids in the neighborhood loved coming over to play. After all I had the coolest dad around and everyone knew it. That was cool shit! I really need to talk about my father so I can truly understand what happens to a person to cause them to want to leave a man for another woman.

When there is no serious reasoning. Now before I continue I must say that of course I was 12 years old at the end of their marriage. But I still know what I saw and heard as a child, nothing made sense to me. As a grown woman now I still can't see it. In this chapter I really do not want to stress the issue much further. I still have other chapters where these things will be discussed.

CHAPTER 2

Being a child adolescence

In my opening statement in this chapter, I need to note that being a child, let alone adolescence is one thing to deal with but having to deal with it through a divorce and dealing with one of your parents being (gay) is the ultimate. Lets' start out with your 12 year of age and your hormones are going crazy and our trying to figure it out. Life begins to be different from when you were younger everything seems so crazy. I know when I was 12 years old I felt alone sometimes especially after my parents divorced.

Prior to that there was always that bonding time with my father and my brothers, mom and me really never had a mother and daughter relationship. I mean in terms of real quality time. We had rare moments of discussion and you know the basic things, but never any of the things I really needed to hear. Liz which was her wife was really the one I could go to and talk about issues that bothered me. I really do not want to touch on that too much in this chapter. There will be time to discuss all of those good things that happened while Liz was in her life.

I remember growing up in my neighborhood all of the cool kids that were around and the ones I really got close with. All had the ideal family, mother, father, sister and brother etc. So really that was all a child needed to know and feel safe. Really being a child it is the duty of the parent or parents if you will that are supposed to protect you from things that are out of sequence. Meaning that any foreign object that is in the physical realm of life. Need I say this book is not based upon any references from growing up in a family who not only had a bad divorce situation, but a gay experience in terms of my mother being gay? So everything that I write about is just from my own experience and nothing more.

For me being a child was like syrup to a pancake just perfect! No worries no care, all you had to do was go to school and be obedient. I mean hell, what more to ask for. Sometimes I often wonder if the adult forgets the concept of children or even raising them. To this day I often wonder why people choose to have children if you can't love them the way the child needs to be loved. Children are different than others. I see that from my own life. The kids I grew up with all had their own personality, that's for sure!

You know parents of all generations, ages, ethnic back grounds etc. are from the same source that used them to get the child here. So when the child gets here, why is it that the parent tends to forget that they were once children and if your parents i.e., parents did the right thing by the child then why can't the same be true for that particular parent. My mother was very good at protecting us from the bad jams of the world, at least

I thought. She was very good about being honest on sexuality except her own.

When she brought a female into our home and began to have the same type of relationship she had with my father, that was, a hard piece of candy to chew! You are looking at things from a different perspective and you begin to wonder if there is something wrong with you. "A very strange way to think" So with all due respect for my mother I don't think she really meant to do us any major harm. Talking with other siblings they feel very similar. The problem with being so young and that lifestyle is forced on a child at such a tender age, can break you, or make you if you will let me explain.

First let me make it clear, this is from my own personal knowledge and no other. What I would like to do is break it down in two categories. (1.) The breaking – Tearing down anything from a child and nor giving the child a chance to breath and understand can be very painful. (2.) The making – Giving the child an education early on about difficulties in like, that we sometimes cannot understand, but at the same time learning to go beyond coping and turning it into a learning experience. Let's examine.

(A) The breaking – We all know to break something means to destroy or try to destroy. Tearing it down as if there is no meaning to it, not caring or believing in it. We get mad at things in our lives or situations so we look for something to break to help ease the pain of our own anxieties or our pains in life. So we look forward to breaking something whether it is important to us or not. We can and will break it. Now you have a material object that I like to call a non-spiritual concept of matter. For some of us these types of objects are very important and on the other hand you have a mind. Spiritual concept of matter which we call humans, not too farfetched anyhow, that kind of object can break as well as the material object that was created by mom. So what am I saying, I am saying although there are 2 types of material that can be broken. Whether it's the kind man created, or the one God created, they can still be broken. I really mean broken in the same way you would throw that favorite crystal glass across the room because you are so pissed off at someone or something! The difference is that the man made material can't feel anything you feel it, because you begin to feel foolish and frustrated because now you lost something that may or may not have been of value to you but now it's too late, it's broken. So maybe for a brief moment the person who threw the object is broken as well.

(B) The making – Let's talk about making a cake. Having all the right ingredients to make a perfect cake. (In your eyes of course) The making of a great cake having the perfect flour, the perfect eggs, at a certain room temperature and all of the other things that go into creating what you need to be a perfect cake. You know all of the ingredients must have their place and time of creation, not anything different from the creator putting all the right ingredients together to create a perfect storm. Well it's almost the same way in the making of a great mind. Teaching the young mind proper educate, understanding emotions and other people and their emotions. Loving, living, laughing and the difficulties that can and will happen in one's life. No matter the age of the child. We all go through life's difficulties; the problem is being able to challenge yourself. What I am saying. I'm saying that it doesn't matter about the color, the creed or the difficulties of the person life it's about how you overcome them and what you have learned from them. I always like to make sure that I know that we as humans have to take our own actions and be accountable for them and not to blame others for their mistakes. So you can see that the making and breaking of an individual is quite relative.

CHAPTER 3

My mother and father (A Relationship)

A s I write this chapter, I often wonder if this book will turn out to be more of a diary than a book. Even if it turned out that way it would be perfect for me after all it is my journey and with the hope of helping someone else with their journey. I had a very interesting conversation the other day that will make this chapter a lot easier to write. I mean it wasn't anything deliberating just interesting. My mother and father as I said before were very sharp people in their own right. They were never abusive to us, not that I knew anyway, but I can say that my mother at times her abuse to me was more verbal than anything.

You know as a child you really did not think that some of the words that came out of a person's mouth can be very abusive especially if you are not aware of the signs. My mother was one you always needed to keep her happy and not piss her off. My father on the other hand was pleasant, calm and very humorous. These are the things I remember in both of them, of course there is a lot more. But I wish not to go too far in that too soon. The couple appeared to be happy at least to a child because as a child you are not to get into your parents space, without a question that is for sure!

Unless you are brought in you stay back and let them be parents. I really choose not to go too far into their relationship without asking the reader to really have an open mind about what a relationship to them. A relationship to me is one that is based upon love of course and kindness for one another and of course respect and integrity. Unfortunately a lot of that is not taking place. We focus more and more on the physical side of things than the relationship. You always hear what can you do for each other to make it work or at least finding out the deeply embedded scars that one can withhold inside that we feel ashamed of being to the service. If we could just take a look at our own self first and then start to do some comparisons I think that we as humans could be on to something. I really want to focus a little more on the mother and father relationship that I saw as a young girl and what I thought was pretty dam normal!

They appeared to be like any other couple on the block, of course on the surface they were married 12 years now that is enough time to figure it out! Why stay were you are not happy? Do it for yourself, not for the sake of a child. I found that in my first marriage that it was a difficult thing to end a relationship when there are children involved, but I believe if you sit down with your child or children and explain to them not your personal reason's but enough so that they have the chance to try and understand, then I think you may be on the right track.

Cold turkey is a bitch! Especially as a child as I said before I didn't want to get too caught up in this chapter about their relationship. I just want the reader to get some kind of insight into a relationship that of course, I thought was ideal. I wanted to keep this chapter brief but informative. In the next chapter I want to take the reader by the hand so that you can see why everything was so difficult to understand as a young girl.

CHAPTER 4

A relationship gone sorrow, the divorce!

As I write in this chapter just one week ago, my mother has passed, I know she is in a good place and my thoughts will always be with her. Now I can begin to tell what needs to be told about the relationship between two people. I remember as a little girl how they would interact with one another. It all appeared to be wonderful; the only thing that was strange to me is that they only would be loving when times were good. Not too far-fetched for a lot of us.

My understanding of relationships is so profound that it may make even the most of us shake! But that is not what this book is about. My understanding of a relationship is in numbers: to me it's about,

(1) Loving

(2) Sharing

(3) Caring

(4) Communication

(5) Honesty

(6) Through thick & thin

(7) Building

I like to call these the seven virtues of a relationship and in those seven virtues I am going to break them down in terms of my mother & fathers relationship that I saw, please let me take you by the hand!

Let's start out with loving and what I saw in them as far as love is concerned. I remember on Christmas night, they were having the best with us kids and they were enjoying their cocktails they had. They had been out all day shopping for the holiday's spending money etc. We always seem to have great holidays together, but it seemed to me that there was another agenda going on. I mean you only love someone during the holidays! If things did not go well with her it was fucking hell to pay!

I remember after we all were off to bed, my mom worked nights dad worked during the day so he was always with us, no dought about it, the man was there. She came home that particular night and was going the fuck off as if the world was at end. She would call my father no good motherfuckers and you sorry son of a bitch! If you will, this was done late at night while we sleeping. So everyone had to wake up and listen to this shit! It was hell at times. That to me did not appear to be much love, not talking to this person about things like ok the light bill was late, or the water bill was late. I mean she worked also; my mother had very, very expensive taste! My father on the other hand was more conservative. That didn't mean a dam thing to her; she needed more, more each time. If you really love someone you work it out. Love doesn't hurt not like that, and love is not selfish. To me that relationship was very selfish.

CHAPTER 5

The meeting of a new partner (very scary)

As I write this chapter, please keep in mind the importance of having an open mind. This book will really make sense to the reader if you allow yourself to have an open mind. The meeting of these two people was very interesting. She, I mean my mom's partner Liz was already in the family. She was married to my mother's cousin at the time; also my mother was married to my father at the time. I was 8 years of age when Liz came into the family from my mother's 1st cousin, who has passed years ago. We really grew to love Liz a lot, she was very pleasant to be a round and she was very sweet and very innocent.

Like I said she was 19 years of age, and just like any young girl she was wanting away out from home. So she married her husband whom was gay also, yes I said gay also! They stayed together for a few years, and then they adopted a son who turned out to be an awesome person! He is a brother of mine; I wouldn't have it any other way. I was only 11 years old at this time and I saw my mom and Liz's relationship get stronger and stronger.

By that time Liz had some of her siblings move to Minneapolis were we lived at that time and all of the girls if you will, started hanging out! They all children so of course we all hung out together! Me being the oldest of the young boys I had to look out for them when the ladies decided to go out for their party's and whatever else they did. It was my younger brother Edward and Liz's son Damian and thus her sisters son Anthony and then me the only girl ha ha we had fun! We got into things just like any child would. At that time it seemed to me that my mother had her face so far into Liz's face, that she forgot all about her children, her marriage, and even herself that it totally destroyed her family. I really don't want to stress too much in this chapter, but I felt it necessary for the reader to understand how they met.

CHAPTER 6

No communication with children, a relationship gone sorrow

By this time in my mother's relationship with her partner, things were really just about her and her partner. By that time I must have been around the age of 13 the prime time of a teenager's life. 13 is a very vulnerable time of life, it's a very crucial time in a young person's life. That age for me was starting to like the opposite sex, wanting to have sex and exploration of a young life, which was very important to me. Not having my mother around to really get close too and bond and create the kind of relationship that begins when you are so young, that was very important for me. At that time my two older brothers were basically out doing their own thing and my younger brother was pretty much on his own.

I can honestly say I spent more time with my younger brother than his own mother spent with him. Not having a father figure in the home, and the two older boys were out doing their thing that was crucial. The absence of a father when there are children around can be very dangerous, especially when there are younger children around. I truly mean this, because I have often seen in my own life the pain that it can cause and the emotions that are so negative, more so than positive. It appeared to me as a young girl, being very close to my father and all the positive things that went around me when he was there, that when he was no longer around it created an atmosphere that was very dangerous in my new environment!

My thought pattern began to change, I even started to look different, and that was very scary. When you have someone in your life that you trust and respect and then all of a sudden they are gone. My father was so hurt behind the breakup that he eventually stopped coming around and that was very painful to all of us! The emotional trauma that is caused often in the family home after a divorce often feels like World War 2, someone just came in and took a person out! My feelings on that are based upon my experience only. I have talked to others on this subject and they are often clueless on just exactly how to feel. I must say that when I started this book I started to write out of anger. I sat on this for 2 years and now I am back at this and will finish out of love.

CHAPTER 7

The disconnection of family, dealing with the shame

To the reader, I must start out with letting you know that dealing with a gay parent in the 1970's and even today if you will, it can be very emotional because of the shame that comes with it. Let me tell you, it was often rough. I remember very clearly how my two older brothers would have the occasional fights when my parents were still together! Boy that was something; I mean they would literally go at it. And me and my other two brothers would just look and laugh, and sometimes watch out to see when my parents would arrive home.

That's when the fights would start when they left the house. So whatever they had stirred up inside before my parents left the house it would come out afterwards when they left to run errands. After the breakup of my mother and father the two older brothers really got disconnected, they were never home and family dinners together just did not seem the same. When my mom's partner moved onto the house, the whole family structure started to change.

My friendships with the kids in the neighborhood that I played with even started to change. I felt this strange feeling of shame, as if I were the one guilty of a sinful crime! That feeling toke along time to go away. It was a feeling that I would not want my worst enemy to feel. Not that I had any enemies at that time in my life. People began to look at me different. My friends would come over and often they would ask questions. They would ask questions like why your mother is sleeping in the same room with your aunt. If she is your aunt why do they share the same room and why are they in the nude with each other?

These are questions that at thirteen years of age I should not need to answer. Nor should they even be asked! For me as time went on I went on. Over the years the agony of that relationship became something in the back of my mind. I no longer stayed in the little shelter that I found myself indulging in. I would stay closed up in my room doing things like listening to my favorite singing groups and getting plenty high! I smoked a lot of pot in those days and the funny thing about it my mom knew I was smoking and that wasn't a problem for her.

So of course my close friends always wanted to hang out at my house. They seemed to have more freedom behind my closed doors. I sometimes often wonder if that is why I did not do my body harm by engaging in a lot of drugs. I believe that fact that she gave us a little more freedom after her divorce from my father. That was not expected but I think that played a major role in that respect. Why me and my younger siblings did not become addicted to any drugs or alcohol to deal with her sexual choices! That was a blessing. But if you ask me, I think it was in the master plan to get through it without using narcotics. The use of drugs would have made things worse. But time goes on and so does life.

CHAPTER 8

Moving on, the later years

As I write this chapter I must say, I am feeling very good about this. As I grew, and not just in a physical sense, I grew in an emotional sense as well. I believe the latter is better! Moving on, life is has been wonderful I still had shaky ground with my mother later in life. I don't think it had to do with her being gay. I know there are a lot of challenges that go along with it. Having a parent who is gay can be intoxicating if you let it. I never wanted to have a toxic relationship with her and a lot of it I'm sure had to do with her not having the skills as a mother to a daughter to ensure me that things were ok, or that things could and will get better.

Later in life I had met someone at the age of 16 and married him at 20 and had 3 beautiful children. My mother was very happy with her grandchildren. I believe it gave her a sense of some kind of security as far as being a grandmother, and she was a very good person to them. Her partner Liz was also a very good person to my children. People would say how do your children react towards your mother and her partner? My comment to that would be like, my children are my children, and they are not my puppets, they are not my dogs, they are people just like me and need to have their own sense of self.

They are people who will get and have the necessary understanding of what's around them. Also it is my responsibility to help them understand any situation that is put onto them. I never forced anything on them in terms of my mother relationship. They saw what was normal to them and they knew that I had respect for her and I loved her. So automatically they returned the same affection. I never once came to them and said oh by the way my mother is gay and this is a very bad situation! It was never discussed in that manner.

Now when they became a certain age they would ask questions and that was fine. They knew she was gay and that it was a different lifestyle then the normal, but they loved there grandmother and had respect for her and her partner. Often times when you have another side of family, and they may have a different perspective on a situation, and I am sure such was the case with my kids but they loved her. The problem with that is my mother really didn't love herself enough to really get down with helping her children understand what was going on with her. I mean it is one thing to be gay and another thing when you are in a normal relationship with a man, and then you decide to go into another with the same sex and not explain to your children not just so much why, but how or what happened.

It really didn't need to be extremely graphic, just some understanding. Moving on, the marriage between me and my children's father dissipated, and we went our separate ways. So dealing with a gay mom, and divorce was a very challenging time in my life. It could be very difficult sometimes when your mother of father is gay, or shall is gay mom this time because I am talking about my situation.

It was sometimes very hard to understand where she was coming from in terms of her helping me get through my times with my ex-husband because she was basing my life off of what was going on in her relationship, and that was unfair to me. It was very apparent that she had some serious issues with men. These things where never discussed; only when she talked about her first husband, and the abuse she went through. That was the only time she would get into it about her life.

She never really would discuss why she became gay! To me if men were so bad then why marry two of them! I have to explain a little here that I am in no way blasting my mother or hating her. I think that when we have children who did not ask to come in this world, it is a responsibility to help your child understand and to help them deal with the critics because they are out there! Back then and even till this day.

CHAPTER 9

The after math losing a partner and a friend

As the years went by, things seemed to have gotten better, I have moved on, and got remarried. She was very pleased with my new husband, of course he was in the military, and she had been in the military as well. Things seemed to improve with my relationship with my mother, but there were always flash backs! What I mean by that is she would always go back in time when things would get a little uneasy with our relationship. She would go blasted on me, and start talking about things like, you don't love me, and you don't respect me!

Man I tell you the shit got wild. I never let those things or accusations control my feelings towards her. It was like she would completely blackout and forget about all of the things that where good between us. She would always express (you don't love me) that became a large impact in her life, believing that! And of course it was so far from the truth. Moving in, as the years went by Liz her partner became ill. She developed cancer and that was devastating for all of us, but she prevailed and made it through. Mt mother and her partner got married, and did not tell anyone!

That was another issue that I had with her, but only for a little while. I remember she and Liz came to visit us in Texas where we were living at the time and we all went out to dinner for a relaxed family time and I saw this ring on her finger and I about flipped out! I didn't say anything to her at that time. So I waited to see if she would say anything to me about it. I felt like, you are still keeping me out of your life in away a stranger would to someone on the street!

I mean I am your daughter; you have been in that relationship for some years now I may not agree with it, but you are still my mother and I do love you! The shit hurts! I think she felt that if no one would agree, then we won't tell them about any of our events, I mean she would tell some of her friends but not her own daughter! With all that said, I realize we can't change a person or there events we can only control our own.

That same time when she was visiting she and I were outside one night sitting by the pool having a conversation about someone a (male) who decided to have a sex change. I thought why are we having this conversation that was really out of me league, if you will. She and Liz were so confident in that discussion that I had to stop it for a moment. The conversation was calm, but I let her know how exactly I felt about it. The next morning when everyone got up she and Liz were in a hurry to get on their way. They were on their way to a family reunion in Atlanta.

I called her while she and Liz were on the road and things seemed to be ok, they were not. She pretended to be ok but she wasn't. Later that day I tried to call her, she wouldn't answer her phone I knew than that she was very upset over the discussion we had the previous night. When they arrived to their destination I Atlanta they were both in a file mood and took everything out on Liz's family. Mt mother had told everyone what was said and that I am homophobic, and that I was wrong in my thinking! (Really) was my response after I had heard what she had said, and basically lied about.

When someone talks about a phobia that means you are afraid of something. Something perhaps of the unknown. Well with that said I fear no one and the fact that she was gay was out of my reach. There was nothing I could do about it! I believe that was one of the main factors, or shall I say problems in my relationship with her. It was never a conversation about how I felt it was about what she thought. I know now that I was not the only person in the world who had to deal with a gay parent that was so confused at times, and unsure about life and themselves.

I finally realized that it was time for me to move on with my life. As time went on so did life. Liz became sick again, Her cancer had returned and things began to go downhill for them. She and I had not talked for over 2 years and within those 2 years my mother lost her partner of 45 years or more. For me I felt like I lost a friend, I know they did not think so but it was true. My mother began to feel the extremes of depression. We finally spoke to one another after the loss of her partner, and it seemed as if things would be ok but I knew better. When we started speaking once again she began to do what she was very good at. She became very distant again and mind you, this was a year after Liz's death.

She really went off the deep end. I surely thought she would be as strong as she professed to be. She started in on me and my other siblings, we don't love her, and we never did etc. She became very ill over this. And told me that she is on her way out and that it is too late for us to begin a relationship. That was very painful; I guess the only true thing in her life was her partner and without her nothing else mattered. Four months later she was gone. My mother had too many things in her life that she made no good! So as far as I am concerned she committed suicide! That was, and is very unfortunate. May God rest her soul?

CHAPTER 10

How I became free from her sexual choice
(living in peace)

Here we are at last! The end game. How I became free from my mother's sexual choice. Number one, I had to realize that it was just that, her choice not mine. Al of the other things in her life were related to her and only her. When we realize that we cannot change a person, a person is responsible for their own change. Then we ourselves become super human beings. Meaning we have created our own inner change. We have set ourselves free from worry, from embarrassment and confusion. You become extremely free as a person.

There is nothing so wonderful when you are free from emotional attachments that we cling onto for our parents and their decisions. I finally realized that she made choices based upon what she felt, and what she knew and not anything against her children. I know now that she really didn't know how to explain her when it came to her relationship with her partner. I know that had to have been extremely hard to explain!

Back then and even now. I also realized that we as a people have to learn to understand our own faults yet alone someone else's. Once people can understand Heterosexuality, then we may understand Homosexuality! But first things first.

In conclusion, I must say to the reader, everything moves for a reason. Nothing will ever stay the same. I remember hearing someone once say you are either getting better or you are getting worse, nothing stays the same. In that respect, if you have experienced a mother or father being gay, let it go. You must learn from it and embrace it or shall I say embrace them. If they have done nothing but loved you, and protected you that was a choice they made in their own lives.

Love them back, respect them and create a wonderful family and life with them. My mother is no longer here in this world, but I know she is somewhere safe. Unfortunately me and my mother didn't get it right between us but I know now that I have to keep it right in my own life. God knows I loved her very much and its ok. I had to move on to my next chapter in life and keep it moving. I have children of my own and a wonderful husband of 30 years and life is wonderful. I miss my mother and all of the wonderful talks we had. Those things will always be with me.

ABOUT THE AUTHOR

Beverly Nimke is an empowerment specialist and she focuses on helping people not cope but live in harmony with themselves. She has 25 years of research and studying Humanity independently. She has found a wonderful secrete in life. She is a mother of 3 adult children and a grandmother of 1. The wife of a retired United States Marine. They currently live in Texas.

To my mother

R.I.P.

Betty Thomas

You will always be loved!

Printed in the United States
By Bookmasters